I'm Already Tucked In!

by
Bil Keane

FAWCETT GOLD MEDAL • NEW YORK

"Hello, Mommy? Could I have a banana?"

"That's a BACK scratcher, Jeffy."

"Barfy and Sam wear flea collars. Couldn't
WE have mosquito collars?"

"I can't finish this soup. It's too deep."

"Look at it this way — Erma Bombeck would
probably find something very
amusing about this."

"This ball has an equator!"

"Why was the commercial so long?"

"Not so loud. You'll wake Daddy."

"Y'know that big window at the church with
the color pictures on it?..."

"Mommy, when you get old how many grandchildren are you gonna have?"

"I'll never understand girls if I live to be 13."

"Will you pioneers turn off the TV set and go to sleep?"

"Was it a very big shoe or were they just
tiny people?"

"You missed a good game, Mommy! First, Dolly spilled her soda, and Jeffy dropped his money under the stands, and I fell outta my seat. . . . Then, in the SECOND inning . . ."

"My peas are tryin' to get away."

"Mommy, why did God invent 'skeetos'?"

"This water's too cold. I'm going ashore."

"Hi, Daddy! I was just gettin' this for you."

"Want me to help you pick up your toys?"

"Why do they hafta put all the good views on top of hills?"

"We made it up ourselves. You don't need nine guys on a team, or grownups, or uniforms. . . . It's like baseball, only better!"

"Careful drivin', Daddy! We don't want you to get dead!"

"Smile, Mommy!"

"Daddy, am I a bachelor yet?"

"But I don't WANT hair on my chest!"

"It's hot as WHAT out today?"

"Can I have one, too?"

"Who taught Barfy how to doggy paddle?"

"Why does Dolly have a top to her bathing suit and I don't?"

"Will somebody help me get my lightning bugs
back in the jar?"

"I saw that in 'The Wizard of Oz.'"

"Pass some more cars, Daddy, so we can wave at them."

"I'll remember where we're parked, Daddy.
It's area Z."

"Mommy! You're always tellin' us not to walk
in the street!"

"If I get lost I'll come back here to wait for you. Could I have a dollar just in case?"

"What kind are you getting for yourself,
Daddy — the mouse ears, the feather,
or the Donald Duck kind?"

"If Sleeping Beauty isn't awake nobody has to
kiss her, do they?"

"Billy! Dolly! Stop playing on the stairs!"

"I don't like to get my head underwater!"

"Know what Billy said, Mommy? He said we have to take off all our clothes 'cause this is a nudist colony."

"How can that mountain have snow on it in August?"

"Look, Daddy! My head's touchin'! I'm tall enough!"

"PJ didn't mind the hippos. The gun shot scared him."

"Know what? Daddy likes this music better than the Bee Gees!"

"Wouldn't you rather go on the Dumbo ride or
Peter Pan? The lines are shorter."

"Poor Mommy. She has to sit over there on
that bench in the shade with PJ."

"Daddy, which coupon do you need to go to the bathroom?"

"They have LOTSA animals here! Why couldn't we bring Barfy and Sam?"

"Next, let's go hear the Matterhorn."

"It was there, Mommy, in the mirror! Right between Daddy and me — A REAL LIVE GHOST!"

"Not 'till after we've gone on Mr. Toad's Wild Ride."

"Don't stand here with me, Daddy. I can drive this one myself!"

"Daddy likes to go on the benches best."

"We have to ride the trolley to use up our "A" coupons."

"Are we back in the United States now?"

"I bumped my elbow and now my arm feels dizzy."

"A lady keeps tellin' me to hang up and dial again."

"I finally found what was causing that awful smell. Billy forgot he stowed a starfish in the tire well."

"Can we go back to Disneyland to use up the coupons we have left?"

"Daddy said he was gonna take a cat nap,
but Kittycat never sleeps like THAT."

"Mommy! It's that lady who talks too long!"

"My mother was lucky. She WALKED to school."

"I don't care WHAT Miss Johnson said about cholesterol. Eat the egg."

"Doctor Ward is a good dentist. He always has the latest comic books."

"Remember when we were anxious for her to learn to talk?"

"We learned about bears on 'Animal Kingdom' and they don't eat porridge."

"What do you say, Jeffy?"
"Wow!"

"Mommy! I just won some dance lessons! Do I
HAFTA take 'em?"

"But, a little while ago you said you weren't gonna ask me to clean up my room again."

"I gave you a cookie a little while ago."
"But my tummy already forgot it."

"Don't put her down on the carpet. She's not housebroken."

"Why must you always be a bad guy?"

"Anyhow, I used to be somethin' none of you
guys ever were — an only child!"

"Every time somebody ding-dongs the door,
Barfy woof-woofs."

"Daddy has my picture in his wallet, so I've got his in my lunchbox."

"What do you want to be when you grow up?"
"Tall enough to reach things without standing on a stool."

"Miss Johnson thinks she knows my trouble.
What does 'hereditary' mean?"

"Jeffy's going to pour the cereal and I'm going to sweep it up."

"I hope traffic's heavy. I have to finish my homework."

"We're learning cursive in school."
"Well, Mommy doesn't like bad language.."

"I'm gonna fetch a glass of water."

"Go wash the jelly off
your face."

"Why does 'quarter to' mean FIFTEEN minutes? I thought a quarter was TWENTY-FIVE cents."

"Which color crayon do you want to borrow?"

"They're called hurry-canes 'cause the wind goes so fast."

"We're playin' car wash."

"God hangs fruit on trees so it won't get dirty."

"Go to your room! And don't turn on the TV
or the stereo, don't play with your road
racers or the pinball machine . . . on
second thought, go to MY room!"

"The party ended early 'cause Jeffy pinned the tail on Danny's father."

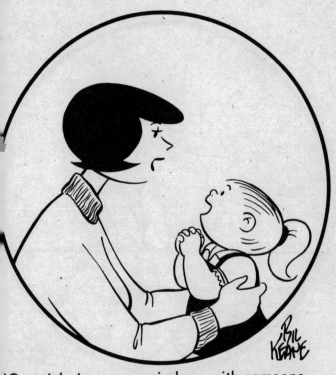

"Certainly I was once in love with someone—
with Daddy!"
"No, Mommy, not like that. I mean REALLY in
love."

"Can't you tune it in any clearer, Daddy?"

"Barfy won't hold his tail still."

"I can't go in the water yet. It hasn't been an
hour since I ate."

"Dolly's not old enough to have her woman's intuition yet, is she, Mommy?"

"Know what, Mommy? I'm wearin' the layered look — a layer of peanut butter, a layer of jelly..."

"I swallowed an orange seed and Billy says
now an orange tree is going to
grow inside me!"

"I'd like to live in this country. It's my favorite color."

"PJ put all the tiddlywinks in my piggy bank!"

"Our bedtime story in a moment, but first, this word about scrubbing our teeth."

"Mommy, am I wearin' a short sleeve or a
long sleeve shirt today?"

"I wasn't asleep. I was just restin' my eyes."

"Did you wash your hands?"
"Who? Me or Daddy?"

"Trees don't need leaves in the winter 'cause
nobody sits under them."

"Now go downstairs and see if you can still smell me."

"This one's on dessert!"

"Do I have to go to college, Daddy? I'm tired of school already."

"Grandma has a new way to do dishes. She
washes them in the sink and dries
them off with a towel."

"How did they know we're not smoking?"

"See? He has a built-in hat."

"The sun is going down into its nest to sleep."

"It's a pumpkin pie, so it doesn't need a roof."

"Well, I didn't have to turn any of our
neighbors into frogs."

"What does 'tch, tch, tch' mean? That's what Grandma said when I walked by."

"Mommy, will you help me put this ketchup back in the bottle?"

"Grandma, when I grow up I'll drive over in
the car you give me to take you
out for a ride."

"Couldn't I have my dessert first just in case
my dinner fills me up?"

"Jeffy, did you take off your muddy boots?"
"Yes, Mommy."

"It's easy to understand why they decided to
give hurricanes BOYS' names."

"I wish Mommy hadn't been deprived of piano
lessons when she was little."

"The worst part about gettin' old is you only get clothes for your birthday."

"Yes, Daddy's here. He's showing everybody his birthday suit."

"Last call! Time for your vitamins!"

ABOUT THE AUTHOR

Bil Keane created **THE FAMILY CIRCUS** in 1960 and used his five children as models for Billy, Dolly, Jeffy and PJ. Today, his grandchildren are his inspiration. THE FAMILY CIRCUS is regularly rated by readers as the number one panel in comics surveys.

●

Bil's brand new strip, **EGGHEADS,** will make its paperback debut with Fawcett later in the year.